# Introverted & In Charge

A Black Girl's HBCU Survival Book

By: Rayvn Webster

ISBN: [979-8-218-73151-9]
Printed in the United States of America.
First Edition: 2025

Cover design, interior layout, and formatting by Rayvn Webster.

# *Dedication*

**For Camryn**

You were the quiet one with the biggest dreams.

The one who was HBCU-ready,

heart full, and ready to change lives as a physical therapist.

The one who did not get to walk across the stage

at high school graduation —

But still inspires every step I take on this journey.

This book is for the girl who did not get to write her college

story — so I'm writing mine and carrying you in every chapter.

Your voice lives on through mine.

Your light still shines.

And every time I speak up, take space, or take a breath, I feel you.

We used to say, *"It's Tea Time."*

Now it's your time —

To be remembered. To be honored.

To live forever through these pages.

I love you always,

Rayvn

# Table of Contents

# Chapter 1: To the Girls Who

# Move in Silence

This book is for the girl with a voice that deserves to be heard.

even if the words get stuck between the mind and the mouth.

It is for the girl who walks into a room and *feels* everything.
The girl who sees it all but says nothing.

The girl whose presence lingers softly but powerfully. The girl
who leaves a mark without ever raising her voice.

This one is for the quiet Black girl finding her way.

Not because she is lost —

But because she is realizing there is
more than one way to lead, to show up,
and to take space.

You do not have to be the loudest in the room to matter.
You do not have to push past your softness to be seen.

This book is your reminder that:

**You have always been enough, even in silence.**

I wrote this book to tell *MY* story — the story of how it felt walking into college as a quiet girl, and how that same college shaped me into the natural-born leader I am today.

Soon, I will be an alumna of **THEE Jackson State University**, a place that did not just educate me but gave me *identity.*

College is not easy when you are shy or introverted. People say, "Just go to school, do your work, and go back to your room." And for a while, I did just that because my room felt safe. It felt like home when everything outside felt too loud, too much, or too unfamiliar.

But college is more than just homework and hiding.

Especially at an HBCU, college is about **becoming**.
Becoming bold. Becoming intentional.
Becoming a *divine Black woman* in your own time and in your own way.

I am here to remind you that you do not have to be the loudest one in the room to be powerful.

You do not have to force what does not feel natural.

Because sometimes, **silence speaks louder than anything**.

So yeah… this ain't your typical college guidebook.

There's no perfect plan. No checklist.

I'm not here to teach you how to be loud, or how to fake confidence, or how to act like you've got it all figured out — because honestly?

**I don't even have it all figured out.**

And you know what?

**That's OK.**

I wrote this from the perspective of a girl who's still learning — still unlearning, still showing up anyway.

The kind of girl who used to shrink herself to fit in, but is finally starting to realize that softness is not a flaw.

Think of me like a big sister.

I've never been one in real life, but this is the version of me I wish had been there when I first stepped foot on campus — someone to say, "You don't have to change who you are to take up space."

That growth doesn't always come with noise.

And that you're allowed to move at your own pace.

At the end of each chapter, you'll find a letter.

Some are to myself. Some are to people I met along the way.

Some say what I didn't know how to say back then.

Some say what I still need to hear now.

They're little reminders that even in the quiet moments, I was becoming.

When you finish the book, you'll find an activity waiting for you, something to help you reflect on your own journey. I even included a playlist and a few scriptures, if that's your thing. Because this book isn't just a guide — it's a mirror, a safe space, a love letter. And with that... this marks the end of Chapter 1.

## *A Letter to My Teenage Self*

You do not have to change who you are to belong here.

You are quiet — and that is okay. You do not have to be loud to be seen, or outspoken to be heard. The right people will feel you without you forcing anything. You are going to find your voice, your place, and your peace in your own time.

You are not behind. You are not invisible.
You're just *becoming.*

Take your time. You are doing better than you think.

**Love,**

**The you who finally**

**understands her power**

# Chapter 2: How to Pick Your Perfect HBCU

*(This choice is about alignment, not aesthetics.)*

I am going to start with a short reflection on how I chose Jackson State University. When it comes to choosing your HBCU, you want to ensure you are going somewhere welcoming, somewhere where you feel like you will be yourself, and it is OK if you feel like you're not at the right school. You either grow into it or you switch. See, college is all about finding yourself, and with that, I would say that my HBCU played a significant role in helping me. I got accepted into over 25+ HBCUs, but I was always a legacy of Jackson State University.

At the time, I was under the influence to go to another school. Still, at the last minute, the day before it was time for me to accept my acceptance letter, I turned around, and I said, "You know what, I want to continue the legacy at Jackson State University."

I'll let you know this: do what your heart desires, not what someone else desires.

You do not have to attend the school that's all about partying. Unless you undergo a 360-degree transformation overnight, you can sometimes feel out of place. I would say the party is a bonus, but you do not have to attend a school that's the most popular or the one seen on the news the most. I love HBCU culture because it just makes you feel welcome. As soon as you touch that campus, it just makes you feel welcome, and that is what I love about it.

You do not have to go to the school that catches the most media attention, or is top in the football game, or has the best dancers, or the best band (shout out to Sonic Boom of the South!)

What matters when picking the right HBCU is going to one that aligns with your personality and your values. Do your research, see what campus culture is like, and check social media to see what students are saying. Not every review or video is going to be perfect, but they are still there for a reason. Attend the webinars, look for safe spaces, and do a tour if you want.

See what the class life is like, see what campus life is about, see what they have to offer — the different organizations, what they do offer for mental health, do the students enjoy it there?
Your heart will tell you what it wants.

Growing up, I was surrounded by people from the alumni. My mother is a graduate of Jackson State University. My dad went to Jackson State University. My sister is a recent alum of Jackson State University [shout out to Class of '25!]. I knew I had an opportunity to either change the legacy or continue it — and I did continue the legacy.

Sometimes when you are in the moment of things, it can feel like a weight of pressure. Like I said before, I had outside voices speaking on where I should go, knowing that my heart was not set on staying in the city or the same state.

Now I'm from Memphis, and everybody I know either went to a local school here or went to Nashville to attend one of the other HBCUs. There is nothing wrong with going to the local, or the community college, or going to one of the other amazing HBCUs, but me personally, I wanted a brand-new, fresh start away from everybody that I either grew up with or got a chance to know. Because college is about a fresh start, and that is what I needed.

At the end of the day, your college experience is yours.
Not your parents', not your counselor's, not social media's.
**You're the one who has to live it.**
So choose a place that feels like alignment — not noise. Not pressure. Not tradition. But *you*.

*A Letter to My Teenage Self:*

Rayvn,

You made the best decision of your life.

You and Rocky are thriving at your HBCU

and I want you to know that

I am proud of you, what you are becoming

and what you have done to mark your legacy here.

Greatness is in your future!

Love,

Rayvn

# Chapter 3: The First Week on the Yard

## (You don't have to do it all to take it all in.)

HBCU Life — being involved in that first week of freshman orientation is truly an experience. When I was in the dorm, they came and woke everybody up at like 6 AM, banging on the doors all loud, trying to get everybody ready. Should have heard my dog — he was concerned. Rocky was going crazy! But it was all about trying to get people out of their rooms and make friends.

Now I already had a few people added on social media from our class page, but I had not met any of these people in person. I already had a few friends from the STEM program that I had completed, so aside from them, I did not know anybody. There were so many different things and activities going on to get everybody involved — and I regret that I hardly went to any of them.

Looking back, it's OK, though. I may not get that time back, but I have made up for it over the years.

I did not make any friends for real during Welcome Week, but I did meet some of my classmates. It was just to get me to try stuff that I never really had a chance to try. I will say it was very inclusive. You had some extroverted and outgoing people, and some shy and Introverted people.

I went to a few events later on, and by a few, I mean two.

When it came to my first week of classes, college was quite different from high school. Back in high school, we had seven periods every day. In college, I had to adjust to having an 8 AM on Monday, then having a 3 o'clock on Thursday, and being done for the week. —vastly different adjustment if you ask me.

But then it's like — what am I going to do after that? Go sit in my room or go outside? Honestly, I chose to go and sit in my room.

I really was just missing home, and everything felt lonely. I just wanted to be with Rocky, and that's it. But that homesickness?

It's universal. Everybody gets it sometimes. I had to learn to adjust to the new space that I was in.

Not only that — I had to get adjusted to classes, but I also had to figure out how to adjust time for eating, when to get snacks, and how to start doing a lot of stuff more independently. Of course, I always had my mom to call, and she has guided me into a thorough source of independence.

But it's like when I got to college — I just froze. It is
like everything she taught me — I forgot.

Honestly, the only time I ever really came out was for food.

Fried Chicken Wednesday and Fried Fish Friday. Y'all, they
always served good soul food — mac and cheese, red beans,
rice and gravy, cornbread, collard greens, red velvet cake, peach
Cobbler, sweet tea, and lemonade. Chileeee, I am reminiscing
because I did not get a meal plan in my second year.

Your first week is what you make it.
You might meet your lifelong friends that week, or you might
not meet anyone at all. That's okay.
Show up in whatever way feels right for you. Just try.
Ease in if you need to. Take breaks when you need to.
But also — keep your eyes open. They usually pass out free
food, T-shirts, water bottles, and snacks, and I know you're
gonna need something to stash in that dorm room for late-night
hunger strikes. Plus, who doesn't like free stuff?
So go for the experience and the free stuff. You deserve both.

## *A Letter to My Teenage Self*

You were overwhelmed. Anxious.

Homesick. But you did not let that stop you.

You kept showing up

 even if it was just to the dining hall

for a plate and a moment of peace.

You adjusted.

 Slowly. Silently. Strongly.

You did not need to go to every party or talk to every person.
You made space for yourself.
And in time?

That space made room for others to find you, too.

I am proud of the girl who did not try to be anybody else.
I'm proud of the one who gave herself grace while growing.

You did not rush it.

You let it unfold.
Now, you have bloomed.

Love Always,
**Rayvn**

# *Chapter 4: Dorm Days & Minded Business*

## *Business*

*(Protecting your peace starts at the door.)*

Every roommate is not the perfect roommate.

I will say this again — EVERY ROOMMATE IS NOT THE PERFECT ROOMMATE!!!

 Sometimes going into college with people that you have known from high school and deciding that y'all are going to room together is not the best decision. My rooming situation going into college was vastly different. I could choose if I wanted to have a roommate or not — and I chose to have a roommate (which did not last long). Whole time? I did not want this girl as a roommate, but that is another story for another time.

My dog was my roommate for my first year of college. I stayed in an ADA room because my dog is an emotional support animal. So, I went through every regulation and every rule and followed the guidelines. I was just a girl with anxiety (VERY BAD ANXIETY), who just needed her dog to get by day-to-day. I told my mother that I was not going to leave her house if I could not take Rocky with me.

So yes, Rocky and I both attend our Divine HBCU, and it is amazing.

Now, do not get me wrong — I have had roommates before when I went on trips or when I went to boarding school for two summers. But from what I have learned with having roommates or sharing spaces is that you must set boundaries in the beginning. I only had a roommate for like two days during college, my first year, and then she left. Other than that, I was alone for the whole school year with my dog — and honestly, I did need that. Not a lot of people get to be that lucky.

If your roommate comes in at all hours of the night, figure out their schedule, and y'all can get together and try to work around it. When it comes to noise, tell them to go to the study room or put their headphones in. There are a lot of things you can do to avoid conflict. Trust and believe housing is a universal issue everywhere, so they do not have time to move you with a new roommate (they will FINE y'all account and go about the day)

Dorm drama is real. It is very, very real. Sometimes, RAs can only do what they can do. Sometimes the RAs and CAs are no help at all. You can either get in cool with them or just go about your business.

At the end of the day, the best advice I can give you is:

- Before you leave your room to go on vacation or anything — take pictures.
- Get dorm insurance. You do not know who will set off the sprinklers in the dorm.
- Set Rules from the Start!! Do not wait till the middle of the year to say something, this is your space too!!
- If you do not like something, speak up!! Set boundaries, use your voice!!
- Do your part!! If you know it is your turn to clean the toilet or take out the trash, just do it!! (Don't be Trifflin')
- If you are having a roommate issue, document EVERYTHING IN BLACK AND WHITE (Email! Email! Email! Have proof and bring receipts!!!)

You have a voice, honey. If you are uncomfortable with something that your roommate does, say something. If your roommate is having guests over and you really do not want to have people in the room, say something. It is not an entitlement. It is called being in a space that you are comfortable in.

Let us talk about how the transition from being in your room back home is different in college. You are living next door to people. Yes, the walls can be thin, and you do hear things. But to be honest, like I said — my headphones are on, and I go about my business. Those dorms can get very depressing, and it can also be a mental drain. Some days, I did not even want to walk back to my room because I was just so cooped up in there all the time.

Also, when you are rooming with people, you must remember — not everybody grew up like you. Not everybody was raised the same.

Not everybody has the exact boundaries and morals. Establish that in the beginning. If your roommate is being unpleasant, do not talk about her behind her back. Just say something. But do not overdo it. You have shared responsibilities. Establish who cleans what all in the beginning.

Do not wait until the last minute and then get mad because you did not say anything. Don't let stuff build up until it turns into a whole situation.

Please get to know your roommate — like seriously.

Y'all don't have to be best friends, hang out 24/7, or even follow each other on Instagram. Be mindful, this is someone that you are going to be sharing a space with for the next few months. The very least y'all can do is be respectful.

Have a quick conversation, learn their vibe. Speak up early if something's bothering you, and try not to make things awkward by letting petty stuff build up. You'd be surprised how far a little communication can go.

Because nothing's worse than living with someone you don't talk to.

No tension, just awkward silence

So, save yourself the headache, Boo.

Say" Hey" and set the tone.

You never know — that "random roommate" might just be someone you needed to cross paths with.

And if not? Cool. Y'all still gotta share a room.

Act accordingly.

### *A Letter to My Teenage Self:*

You learned how to hold your space.

How to protect your peace.

How to speak up when something felt off —

even when your voice was shaky.

You needed peace. You needed quiet. You needed you.

I am proud of the way you made that room a sanctuary.

Of how you learned to say "no" without guilt.

Of how you learned what you needed without apology.

You did not fold. You figured it out. You are home now.

Love Always,

Rayvn

# Chapter 5: How to Find Your People Without Doing the Most

## (Connection doesn't always come from conversation.)

Let me tell you about JoJo. We have had our difficulties, but she remains my homegirl to this day. We are both young black women majoring in Engineering. I have pulled all-nighters with this girl. If you can pass chemistry with your friend?

That is a friend for life.

She is a Gemini, and I am a Sag so of course it balances out.

We met through the same STEM summer program, but we did not start talking until we became dorm neighbors. Rocky loves his Auntie, even though she is allergic to him. Oh, and she is a Mississippi native, so you *know* she gon' tell it like it is.

I also have a whole friend group that came out of that same STEM program. We have been locked in ever since. Sometimes the group chat can be dry, but the love is still there. Mooney, my little brother (who is taller than me) always got my back. Angel, who has since transferred back to Louisiana, remains a massive part of my journey. She is a real one and deserves her flowers. My homegirl Tankey, who is always down for whatever, that is my dawg!!!

You cannot forget Rocky. They all love him.

Disclaimer — not all your best friends are going to come from your HBCU. One of my closest friends, Peaches, goes to a PWI back home. That girl has had my back through thick and thin. When I was in my season of Silence, that girl and I went through it together. I changed my number, fell into isolation, and she stayed solid. We met on social media and have been the best of friends ever since.

Just because you go to school does not mean that people that you grew up with or people that you went to high school with still aren't your friends. I keep up with some people I went to high school with, and we go out to eat occasionally, but you know, Life moved on after we left for college. You're going to meet other people; you're going to meet new people. It's a whole new experience, especially if you're going to an HBCU, you're around people who are like you find your group click with it. You find your real friends when you're in college, and you also keep some friends while you're in college. Did I tell y'all about Sisi? We go way back in the day; that's practically my cousin lol.
But not everybody is your friend.

Like MO3 said,

"Everybody ain't yo' friend

Everybody ain't yo' partna"

Let me say it again: *NOT EVERYBODY IS YOUR FRIEND*

In college, some people will only befriend you because you have a car. Yes, you heard me right. Do not go on that campus offering rides. Do not let everybody ride in that car. Do not be out here giving no rides and not getting any gas money. Tell them you need $10 on the mile up front. A car in college is a lure for people to try to befriend you for a ride to Walmart, lol. Be mindful.

Some people will smile in your face while secretly envying you behind your back. As you grow, you will realize that

Not everyone is meant to go with you.

**You cannot save everyone.**

Eventually, you must learn to stop pouring into empty cups.

You deserve friends who pour into *you.*

*Now that I'm older, I don't feel the urge to be a certain type of way just to have friends. At the end of the day, I am unapologetically me.*

I have met amazing people through travel opportunities,
through orgs I have joined, and through just being myself.

I have met incredible women from other HBCUs. Powerful young
Black men.

Alumni who saw something in me.

Mentors. Role models. Real ones.

Friendship in college is not about the loudest crew or the
biggest group chat.
It is about alignment.
It is about energy.
It is about safety.


Find your people —
even if it takes time.

## *A Letter to My Teenage Self*

You did not know how many people

would love you for simply being you.

You did not know how many real ones

 would show up once you stopped chasing the wrong ones.

You have built a circle. Not the biggest. But the truest.

And now? You do not chase energy.

You attract it.

I am Proud of you Honey.

Love Always,
**Rayvn**

# Chapter 6: Speak Up Without Switching Up

## *(Your voice matters, even if it shakes.)*

As you get older, you learn that nobody is going to be an advocate for you better than yourself. Honestly, that turning point came when I got into college — and it is still something I am continuing to work on. But I am getting better. I am learning to advocate for myself and speak up when something does not sit right.

Your frontal lobe starts to develop, and things you used to find entertaining or acceptable might not feel the same anymore. That is growth. That is transformation. That is what I mean when I say, *"Speak up without switching up."*

You are allowed to evolve. You are allowed to outgrow versions of yourself. But that does not mean you have to mold yourself into a whole new person or copy a personality you saw on TikTok. Be the version of you that *you are still discovering* — not the one that fits into someone else's aesthetic.

There have been so many times I missed the chance to speak up.

I am a go-with-the-flow kind of girl, so I usually let things slide. But I have learned to say something. Even if it is small, like getting the wrong drink. "Hey, I didn't order this." Yes, it seems like such a small thing, but it is a start.

Especially when you are paying for something, you deserve what you paid for.

When I am in new environments, I go quiet. Not because I am mean or standoffish, or because I am better than anybody, but because I genuinely do not know anyone, and it is overwhelming. That silence is not arrogance; it is processing.

But in college, I have learned that communication is everything. Whether it is Welcome Week, in your dorm, at your job, your internship, or during interviews, communication is key.

And the truth is?

The harshest critic you will ever have is yourself.

We hold ourselves back by doubting who we are and what we have to offer. We as people have to learn to be less critical of ourselves.

Finding your voice is a process, but you will get there. You do not have to be the loudest in the room — just make sure that your presence speaks before your words do.

Sophomore year is when I truly found my voice. I started stepping up, doing things I never thought I could. Everything I once thought was out of reach became possible once I stopped doubting myself.

Speaking up? That changed everything.

You may not find your voice first year. It might take time.
And that is okay.

But whenever it comes, use it.

You do not always have to speak first — but speak when it
counts. And if saying it aloud feels too hard at first?

Write it down. That counts, too.

There are also going to be things you used to think were okay that
now feel distasteful — and that is fine.

It is okay to speak up about anything that rubs you the wrong way
if you do it respectfully. Respect goes a long way.

It is earned, not given, but always respect those who respect you.

Come with kindness, and correct people the first time. That is
not being mean. That is just protecting your peace.

## *A Letter to My Freshman Self*

You were so quiet. So observant. So in your head.

But even in silence, you were learning.

You did not need to be the loudest.
You needed to be *heard* — and now? You are.

I am proud of the way you grew into your voice.
You started small but kept pushing forward.
How you showed up, even when you were scared.

You stopped letting people speak for you.
And now? You speak with power.

Always,
**Rayvn**

# *Chapter 7: Reserved, Not Replaced*

*(Your quiet doesn't cancel your greatness.)*

My silence has always been my strategy.
I've learned how to navigate a room without making noise.

The first thing I do when I walk into a space? I find my seat, then I greet.
I do not come in loud or over the top. I come in observant,
looking for familiar faces or someone I might vibe with.

I do not need to do the most to be noticed. I was not in everybody's face, but somehow, I was always in every room.

**Being reserved does not mean being replaceable.**
Just because I stay to myself does not mean I am not qualified.
I'm quiet — not absent. I am soft-spoken — not silent.

When it came to group projects, nobody expected me to take the lead.
But I did. I organized. I researched. I held it all together.

They did not see it coming because I was not the loudest — but I was the glue.
I did not yell. I executed.

People love to mistake quietness for insecurity — but let me be clear:
I am *very* aware of who I am.
Some folks lose interest when you are not constantly talking.

But truthfully? I am just observing.
I speak when I have something worth saying — and when I do speak, it shakes the room.

**Do not take my silence for shyness.**

**At this age, I'm not shy — I am strategic.**

Even in Zoom meetings, I keep that same energy. I do not always unmute.
Sometimes, I am quiet because I am locked in — taking notes, listening, analyzing. I might drop a "good job" or "congratulations" in the chat, but I do not always feel the need to speak.

I am not detached — I am just in my zone.

But when I do speak? I make sure it counts.
I had a major presentation with a Fortune 500 company —

*Rayvn Webster* **had a presentation with a Fortune 500 company.**

Crazy right?

I was the **only** girl in the room.
And I nailed it. I shook the entire room.
They did not expect it. They did not see it coming.

But now? That VP is waiting to send me an offer when I graduate.

I still cannot believe that happened — but I am proud.
Proud that I stepped up. Proud that I spoke up.
Proud that I stayed with myself through the entire process.

I've done so much as a sophomore going into my junior year —
sometimes I forget to stop and reflect. I've moved through so
many chapters, jumped over hurdles I never thought I'd clear,
and said yes to things that once made me nervous.

I didn't just step out of my comfort zone — I grew from it.
I learned that discomfort isn't always the enemy; sometimes, it's
the sign that you're *becoming*.
The world moves fast.
Life… it never stops.

And when you're busy trying to keep up, it's easy to miss how
far you've come.
But every single day holds something worth growing from —
even if it's small.

You're evolving in ways you probably don't even notice yet.
It's okay to pause.
To sit down, breathe, and reflect on your journey so far.
You *deserve* to acknowledge the growth.

Just don't stay stuck in the reflection. Don't let it make you
afraid to move forward.
Because this world will keep spinning.
And you? You're still in it. Still showing up. Still rising.
**I have never been, and never will be, replaced.**
And neither will you.

## *A Letter to My Teenage Self*

You were never invisible.
Even when you did not say much,

Your presence was always known.
I know you questioned it sometimes —

wondered if being quiet made you forgettable.

**But now you know:**

Your silence was never empty.
It was full of observation, full of awareness, full of strategy.

You did not have to compete for attention to be valuable.
You were valuable from the moment you walked in.

I am proud of the way you stayed true to yourself —
how you did not let the noise of others drown out your own pace.

You learned when to speak, how to speak, and most importantly,
you learned that your voice did not have to echo to be heard.

The same girl who used to stay on mute?

She's now walking into rooms and shaking the table.

Not because she changed who she was
— but because she *embraced* who she is.

You have proven that being reserved does not mean being left
behind.
And every time you show up —

 fully, quietly, confidently —
you remind the world that you are here on purpose.

Always,
**Rayvn**

# *Chapter 8: Distractions, Drama, and Knowing When to Log Off*

Now college is not just all education — it is fun and games too. But let me tell you something: distractions, drama, and knowing when to log off are *essential life skills* in this journey.

Yes, you will build academic knowledge, but you are also building your identity. That means having *social relationships*—not just classmates. You cannot just be all school and no play.

If that is your vibe, go for it. But balance is important. We all need to breathe, to laugh, to *live* a little.

You are young, but you are also stepping into adulthood. That means you will meet a *lot* of people. Some will be for you. Others? Not so much. Some of your friends will be in relationships, situationships, sneaky links — whatever y'all call them — and there you are… just out of the way.

And listen, there is *nothing* wrong with that.

There is power in being alone. You do not always have to be with someone. I have seen too many people go back to the one who hurt them or jump into relationships just because "it's college." You do not have to rush. You do not have to force it.

Find *you* before you try to find *someone else.*

Yes, some people meet their soulmate in college. That is beautiful — for them. But your path is *your* path. The first person you meet is *probably not* your forever. Emotional stability matters. Do not try to fix someone when they are not even trying to fix themselves.

That is a burden you do not need.

Stop falling in love in three days and wondering why you are drained by Day 7. These talking stages? Stand on business. And remember — you are not a rehab center for broken people. Be open, yes, but protect your energy.

Let us get into **friendship drama** for a second. I have a story.

Freshman year, I got close with a group of three girls. Something felt off — like nobody else really hung around them. Two of them had nasty attitudes, and I did not click with the third either.

I had a car, and suddenly it felt like that was all I was good for. They never respected my time. One night, a Gospel Explosion event took place on campus. I was excited to go. They said they would come with me, but showed up 30 minutes late.

I waited outside, hoping not to walk in alone. That is when Angel showed up. She was not even dressed for the event, but she offered to walk me inside just so I did not feel alone. That is *real* friendship.

Meanwhile, the other girls came in late, sat *behind* me, and started playing around during praise and worship.

I was already battling a tough depression after losing Camryn —
that moment of surrender was real for me. They laughed at me.
That is when it clicked. God gave me a sign.

*Disrespect is a choice. Once is enough. Twice is intentional.*

Let that be a lesson — you do *not* have to tolerate people who
mock your healing or take your peace for granted.

**Set boundaries.** Speak up.

Advocate for yourself — even with your closest friends.

Now, let us talk about relationships again. If you are with
someone, it should *not* feel like survival mode. You should not feel
alone *in* a relationship. You should not feel drained all the time. Do
not confuse familiar with connection.

That is how people stay stuck in cycles.

And please — stay out of your friends' drama.

People are wild these days. Mind your business, stay safe, and stop
getting caught up in a mess that does not belong to you.

Finally: **KNOW WHEN TO LOG OFF.**

One thing I learned from Camryn was the value of mental health
breaks. She would deactivate, unplug, and *recenter*. That is
something I have learned to adopt for myself. As a generation, we
are glued to our phones. We hop from app to app, feed to feed —
and we wonder why we feel drained.

I took an entire year off social media once. Best decision I ever made. No distractions. Just *me*, building myself back up. Mute that group chat if it is stressing you out. Take a break. Reset your mind. Choose peace. Set boundaries. And learn to say **no** without guilt.

So yes, college will come with distractions, drama, and noise. But that doesn't mean you have to lose yourself in the mix.
You have the right to protect your peace.
You have the right to say no to the group chat, the ex, the situationship, the invite, the "friend" who only hits you up when they need a ride.
You are not a fixer. You are not a therapist. You are not a backup plan.

You deserve to be surrounded by people who pour into you, not drain you. Take your space when you need it.

Your world won't fall apart because you took a moment to breathe.
Distractions are loud. Drama is easy.
But discernment? That's powerful.
And learning when to log off is healing.

You don't have to prove anything to anybody. Not by how many people you're around. Not by who you're dating. Not by how fast you respond to a text. Let go of that pressure to be "on" all the time. Rest is productive. Stillness is valid. Sometimes, the most adult thing you can do… is *log out and let it go*.

You're not missing out. What's for you will never require you to shrink, beg, or break yourself to keep it. The right people, the right spaces, the right timing — they all honor your boundaries and your peace. Protecting your energy is not selfish. It's survival. It's self-love.

## *A Letter to My Teenage Self*

You held it together when nobody

saw the weight you were carrying.

You gave yourself room to cry, to pray, to be honest.

You learned what real friendship looked like.

You stopped letting fake ones sit at your table.

You stopped giving.

You started protecting your peace.

You are not bitter. You are *better*.

And your heart still shines.

Always,
**Rayvn**

# Chapter 9: I Don't Party, But I Still Pop Out

## (Presence doesn't require a party.)

You hear a lot about college parties — on TV, in movies — like they are this rite of passage. Real life is nothing like what you imagined watching Stomp the Yard or House Party growing up. I have been to my fair share of parties. I can honestly say I have only really enjoyed two of them. I am talking about the "ladies free before 11" or "$10 entry" type of parties.

Looking back, I wish I had kept that money — because most of them were just... lame.

Half the time, I was only going because my friends wanted to go. I did not enjoy them. I was not drinking, and I was always the designated driver, which did not bother me. It made the whole experience feel even more... pointless.

Let me break it down: a college party, most of the time, is in a rented-out event hall or an abandoned warehouse packed with people — mostly between the ages of 18 to 32 — hot, smoky, reeking of weed and BBL aftercare, and full of folks who don't know how to handle their liquor.

There's yelling, fighting, throwing up... it can get *ghetto* quick.

The only party I liked? An R&B party — because all that loud trap music every five seconds gets overstimulating for me. I hate being touched or bumped into, and I do not like people grabbing me or trying to dance up on me unless we are cool. I know that's part of the party scene, but it is just not for me.

Now, I *do* love a good **kickback**.

When I say kickback, I mean like 10 to 20 people I know. That is not a party — that is a vibe.

That is where I can show up as my full self.

Baby, do not get me started on lounges. I went to one because my friend worked at a lounge, and it was cute and grown, but Auntie still wanted to be in bed by 10:30. I am not with the all-night outside life anymore. I have responsibilities, goals, and a bedtime now.

**Presence is about authenticity, not performance.**
And that is the part a lot of people do not get.

I do not party, but I still pop out. I still show up. I love brunches. I love campus events. I love student org meetings. I love meeting people with a purpose. I show up dressed cleanly, modestly, and confidently. Not because of my body type — just because that has always been my style.

Now, I have tried to switch it up before. One time I wore short shorts to match my friend, but I had a jacket over me the whole night.

It just was not me. But let me tell you something: **your size does not define what you wear.** Wear what makes *you* feel confident.

Do not tailor yourself to fit into clothes — the clothes were made to fit you.

But shout out to the bigger girls on campus who *do* show skin, wear what they want, and look good doing it. Y'all, the reason I started wearing crop tops.

That confidence? I love it. Y'all are beautiful, and y'all inspire me.

Back to what I mentioned in the last chapter — about those girls I used to hang with? Yes, they LOVED to party.] I always felt like I was just there to be the sober driver. One time, one of them got drunk and accused me of wanting her boyfriend, which is *extra funny*, considering I do not even date boys.

They say drunk minds speak sober thoughts... and that insecurity showed loud.

I still drove her home. Because I am not about to argue with anybody drunk and delusional, but that moment told me everything I needed to know.

Let me say this:
**If you are going to go out, know your limits.**

If you are going to drink:

- Keep your eyes on your drink.
- Do not take anything from anyone you do not trust.
- If you came together, *leave together*.

I know people say, "It won't happen to you," but that is not always true. I have never forgotten the case of Kenneka Jenkins. That tragedy has stayed heavy on my heart for years. And that is why even when I want to leave early, I stay because I want to make sure my friends get home safely.

But if you want to stay home? Do that.

If you want to leave early? Do that, too. Just make sure you've got your crew with you. Just remember, **you do not have to go out to stand out.**

Now, that's not to say I won't ever go to a party — let's be clear. I might just pop out on y'all when the vibe is right. I know my social battery, and I'm not afraid to honor it.

So best believe I'll step in, hit my lil move when *Flex by* Cupid comes on, grab a plate, and dip before it gets too loud. I'm not for every scene, but when I do pop out? Just know it's gonna be on my vibe and my time.

## A Letter to My Teenage Self

You thought partying was the way to feel included.
You thought saying yes meant you were showing up.
But now you know — you were always enough,

even when you stayed home.

You did not need the crowd to validate you.
You needed peace.
And girl, you chose it, even when it made you feel alone.

I am proud of the way you looked out for your friends.
Proud of how you stayed true to your spirit.

Now?

You are in your own lane, and it fits you perfectly.
Still popping out. Still present.

Still powerful.

You did not need to party to be seen.
You just needed to be *you*.

Always,
**Rayvn**

# Chapter 10: I'd Rather Love Myself

## (Learning to be full without forcing someone else to fill you)

There have been so many moments where I went out looking for love in other people, only to get back half of what I deserved. Not even half. One-third on a good day. I was out here pouring my whole soul into folks who could barely return a sip. And for what?

I had to learn that real love starts at home—*with me.*

Loving me did not mean having it all together. It meant learning to stop abandoning myself just to keep someone else around. I had to stop showing up for people more than I was showing up for me. That is not loyalty. That is self-neglect.

Yes, I am still that girl who will cheer you on from the crowd, hype you up, and make sure you get the recognition you deserve. But I have also learned to give that same energy to myself. I started setting boundaries, not because I stopped caring—but because I realized some people only know how to take.

And when you are always the one giving? It drains you.

There was a time when I was giving love, advice, and care to everybody around me while ignoring the fact that I needed that same support. I was quick to tell a friend not to settle… meanwhile, I was settling for silence, for confusion, for inconsistency in my own life.

That had to change.

So, I started showing up differently for myself.

Now I take solo walks with Rocky—even if he stops every five steps. I am available for journaling, for poetry, for slow mornings where I speak affirmations over myself. I will say, "You are loved. You are enough. You do not have to shrink."

And I will mean it. I stopped waiting for someone to love me the way I needed to be loved and became the first person to do it.

Self-love became my standard. Not just something cute to say on Instagram—but a daily practice.

That means saying no without guilt.

It means not forcing yourself to stay in places where you are not seen or valued. It means choosing peace over partnerships that leave you confused. Let's be real, college will have you in situationships so fast, you will forget what your own voice sounds like.

Do not fall into the trap of needing someone else to validate your worth.

Because sometimes, the biggest heartbreak is not from losing someone—it is from realizing how long you went without choosing yourself.

And now?

I would love myself. Every time.

Because no one—*no one*—can love me better than I can... except God. We are both rooting for me.

## *A Letter to My Teenage Self*

Hey love,

You wanted so badly to be chosen.
But somewhere along the way,

you forgot you were already worth choosing — by *you.*

You gave and gave. You were the one always pouring,
always checking in, always available.
But baby, who was doing that for *you?*

You learned the hard way that not everyone
deserves a front-row seat in your life.
And that is okay.

It hurt. But it taught you to stop begging for

crumbs when you were the whole table.

I am proud of you for walking away

when you knew it was draining you.
I'm proud of the nights you choose peace

instead of proving your worth.
I'm proud of how you started showing up for yourself the way
you always showed up for everyone else.

You did not need to be loved perfectly —

you just needed to know that you were worth loving at all.

And now? You give that love back to yourself.

Daily. Intentionally. Unapologetically.

Keep choosing you.
Keep loving you.
Keep becoming you.

Always,
**Rayvn**

# Chapter 11: God, Growth & Quiet Time

*"He saw me when I couldn't see myself."*

You do not understand how vital a relationship with God is until you hit your 20s, or until something traumatic rocks your world.

I have always been a Christian. I have always had faith. But I am not going to lie and act like I did not question things, especially when life got heavy.

I used to sit there like, "God, why would you let me go through this? Why me?" I did not realize until later that the things I thought were breaking me were grounding me.

Freshman year hit like a brick.
Seasonal depression, grief, confusion — it was so much.

I had not felt that low since my daddy passed away. Even back then, I did not fully understand how to lean on God. I was

58

still going to church, showing up, but I did not really *get it*.
Not yet.

Then I got to college. I was fresh out of a breakup — which I
should've let go of long before — and I found out I lost Camryn.

My entire world shattered. I started spiraling into unhealthy habits
and surrounding myself with people who did not care about me. I
was just existing at that point. But at night? I felt empty. I was in
a room full of people and still felt like I was all by myself.

I was tired. I was done.
And that's when God stepped in.

Funny thing about God — He will *always* show up, especially
when you do not expect Him. I did this removal prayer I saw
on TikTok.

Just asking God to take away anything not meant for me. And
baby… He did. Quick. Those girls were gone the *next day*. I sat in
silence with God, and I finally felt like I could *breathe* again.

I never lost my faith — it was just running low.
But God always had me.

Sophomore year? That is when my faith got stronger.

Even during another breakup that felt like hell on Earth, I knew I
was changing. I started praying for the people who hurt me. I
stopped holding onto hate. That is when I realized: I was healing.

And let me tell you something — spiritual growth in your 20s is
*necessary*.

I took a break from social media.
I changed my number.
I focused on school, on Rocky, on prayer.

It felt like a full reset. A clean slate.

A brand-new version of me, rooted in peace.

I am not the perfect Christian — but I know in God's eyes, I am already whole. I journal, I walk, I pray before the sun comes up. Sometimes I cry. Sometimes I sit in silence. But I always come back to Him.

God has sent me divine connections, divine downloads, and divine protection. He is the MVP, the one who never left my side.

If there is one thing I have learned, it is this:
You do not have to wait until your life falls apart to run to God.

He is already right there.

**Waiting.**

**Listening.**

**Loving you,**

even when you do not know how to love yourself.

## *A Letter to God*

Thank You for never leaving me.
Even when I pulled away, you stayed.
Even when I doubted, you showed me.

You gave me signs.

You gave me peace.
You removed the things

I did not have the strength to let go of.
You brought me back to myself.

Thank you for the quiet moments.
The stillness. The healing.
For whispering "You're not alone"

 when the world got too loud.

You are my safe place. My anchor.
And I love You for loving me —

even when I did not feel worthy.

Always,
**Rayvn**

# Chapter 12: Quiet Rooms, Loud Moves

One thing I have learned about going to an HBCU is that you do not always have to be loud. You can walk into a room and get straight to work. And what I mean by that is—like I said before—you do not have to be the loudest person in the room to leave a mark.

Quiet does not mean incapable.
Being quiet does not mean you do not have anything to say.

When I am around people I am comfortable with, yes, I might show out. But what about those moments when you are not in a loud scene? What about those silent, awkward rooms where nobody's talking? What do you do when the anxiety kicks in—do you wait for someone else to speak, or do you say something first?

That is the tension of being introverted. Sometimes, I know I give off a vibe that underestimates what I am capable of. But I am still a reserved person. I do not always want to be the first one to speak. I will ease into the conversation. You can either end with me or place me somewhere in the middle, but I would rather not be the opener.

In so many career spaces, they reward extroversion. They reward people who are outspoken, loud, and commanding. But where is the love for the introverts in business, in tech, in leadership?

I am an engineer. Everybody I know in my field is honestly just chill. We are laid-back, we code, we game, and we stay in our own world. That is why I know I am in the right space. It is funny though, because when it is time to pitch a project? You would think we were auditioning for Shark Tank or American Idol (Is that the one with the golden buzzer? Either way... You get it.

You learn to have a *career performance*.
Even as an introvert, you learn how to flip the switch when it matters.

That is especially true with networking. It is everything. Whether you are in business, engineering, psych—or any field—it is how you get jobs, internships, and the chance to grow. That is how you get opportunities to travel, study abroad, or land real career placements. But let me tell you... that was not always easy for me.

My first year was *hard*. I was fighting to rebuild my GPA. My mental health was not the best, so I avoided most campus events. And because I was trying to keep myself afloat emotionally and academically, I did not land an internship for a while. Like, a good while.

I remember going home and just... sitting. I was not working. I was not studying. The job market was trash, and nothing was clicking. I almost gave up. I was *this* close to going to work with my mama and listen—my mama is fantastic at what she does(miss psychology major), but I did **not** want to go work with her. Not because I did not love her, but because my pride could not take it. I did not want to ask for help. I wanted to earn something *on my own*.

That pride? It had me stuck.

Eventually, I said, "If I'm not going to do anything, I might as well try to get better." So, I started going deeper into coding. I studied at night, locked in, and knocked out a new certification in a few days. But even after that, I did not know what was next. I still felt… stuck.

Then, out of nowhere, God came through.

Right when I was ready to give up and tell my mama I had come to work with her, she went to an alumni cookout. And there, she met someone I now call my *uncle*, Dr. Ted. He owns a clinic in our city and helps vaccinate the entire Mid-South. Turns out, I went to high school with his daughter. Small world, right?

Dr. Ted and his family came through in ways I cannot even explain. He created space for me at his company, even though I am not in the medical field. I turned their paper forms into a digital platform. I found my lane and ran with it.

I started that internship on **July 1, 2024**—and it changed everything.

It was my first *bona fide experience* doing something that made me feel valuable. I still go back to help when I can. Even though it is not my industry, they made space for me. They saw me. It is a family-like environment, and I *never* want to leave. That was the start of my growth. That was the moment everything shifted.

And here is the thing:

It happened because someone saw my quiet… and knew there was power in it.

## *A Letter to Myself*

Dear Me,

I know sometimes you feel like you are not doing enough.

Like you are too quiet, too reserved, too unsure.

You question if you are being seen. You wonder if you are falling behind. But look at you.

You have made it through everything that tried to make you feel invisible.

Your silence was never a weakness —

It was preparation. You have been watching, listening, learning, building. And now? You are showing up.

You are not loud, but you are powerful.

You are not everywhere, but when you *are* in the room, you are undeniable.

You did not need a spotlight to grow. You just needed space.

And you have created that space for yourself, little by little, even when it felt like no one noticed.

I am proud of you for not giving up when it got lonely.

I am proud of you for asking for help when your pride did not want you to.

I am proud of you for choosing progress over perfection, and for choosing purpose over pressure.

Keep moving in silence if that is what brings you peace.
Because whether they clap or not, your work still echoes.

And just so you never forget:
**You're not too quiet. You are just focused.**

Love,
The girl who kept going

# Chapter 13: Booked, Busy & Boundaries

Let me tell y'all something: I feel like I have been paving my way and making my mark. In the summer of 2025 alone, I had **three internships**. Three! From the outside looking in, it seemed like I was living the dream, and do not get me wrong, they *were* amazing opportunities. But listen... I do not usually like to say I am stressed, but Grandma was *tired*, okay?

I am still learning how to get more involved on campus while staying true to myself. That is why I intentionally spent the **fall of my sophomore year** being chill and low-key. I needed that time to be still. But by the time **spring** rolled around, I was ready to push myself — to open more, to network, and to step into some rooms I used to fear.

That spring, I started working more, became a research student, and fell in love with the work I was doing.

I got closer with the people in my department, and because of those relationships, I started to get opportunities to *travel, attend summits, go to conferences*, and *meet people I never would have met otherwise*. Networking truly opened doors I did not even know existed.

But with every opportunity comes a lesson:
**Just because it is good does not mean it is good for you.**

At one point, I had so many offers on the table that I just started saying yes to everything. I did not want to miss out. I did not want to seem ungrateful. But that's how burnout creeps in — when you are moving so fast that you forget to check in with yourself.

I remember one internship.

About three weeks in, I had to be real with myself... and them. I told them, "I am sorry, but I don't understand anything. This just is not for me." It was not my lane, and I was trying to force it. When I am not interested, I get bored. When I am bored, I get irritated. Honestly? That is not fair to them or me.

So, I stood on my boundary. I called my mom first, like I always do — and I asked her, "Should I keep this? It is a fantastic opportunity, the pay is amazing, but I am mentally drained. I am not learning anything, and it does not excite me." Her response? Whew. That is why she is the best mom in the world. She said:

> *"Rayvn, you know you best. That is a decision only you can make — but always have a backup plan. If the opportunity is not for you, you will know it."*

And she was right. I knew. So, I thanked them, finished the week, got my last paycheck, and stepped away.

And guess what? **The very next week, I received a $10,000 scholarship** and got accepted into a leadership council. Two blessings I was not even expecting. That is when I knew: *God was working behind the scenes.*

Now, for a moment, I started to regret leaving that internship. It was with another Fortune 500 company, and I thought it might look bad on my résumé. But I had to remind myself — I did not leave because I could not do the work. I left because I chose myself. One of the people I worked with there still checks in and supports my journey. He even told me he is proud of how I stood up for myself.

Sometimes you must ask yourself:

**Are the things I am doing helping me grow, or am I scared to look lazy?**

You do not have to exhaust yourself to prove your worth. Trust me, your work will speak for itself. But *protecting your peace* is a major part of that.

Especially at an HBCU. Especially as a Black woman. There is this constant pressure to be *everything*: smart, social, spiritual, strong. But let me say this one more time, loud enough for the girls in the back:

**You do NOT have to exhaust yourself to prove your worth.**

Boundaries are not selfish. Boundaries say, *"I believe in my purpose too much to let everything drain me before I even get there."* And listen — burnout does not ask for permission. You will be drained over stuff that has not even happened yet.

So, here is how I protect my peace while still staying booked and productive:

### *My Boundaries in Action:*

- **Apple Calendar & Reminders? Lifesavers.** Google Calendar is good too. And if you have Alexa? Use her.

- **Do Not Disturb = Freedom.** I will keep it up. I am reachable to three people. If it ain't my mama, my sister, or my close friend — try again later.
- **Location stays ON.** Not for show, but for safety.
- **I do not attend everything.** If I am not passionate, I am not going. Period.
- **Every "yes" means a "no."** Am I saying no to rest? Creativity? Peace? I weigh it *before* I say yes.
- **Morning and night routines keep me grounded.** I am not perfect with it, but even 30 minutes to myself makes a difference.
- **Take a walk.** I love walking with Rocky (even if I end up carrying him like the spoiled baby he is). Those walks are my reset button.

Peace is my **priority**, not a privilege.

And I do not feel guilty about choosing myself first anymore. That is growth. I get things done. I am still *that* girl. But burnout? That is not in my plan. I do not owe anyone full access to me just because I am capable.

Being strong doesn't mean being available 24/7.
Being dependable doesn't mean being drained.
Being capable does not mean I owe the world full access to me.

I've learned to stop explaining my boundaries to people who benefit from me not having any. I've learned that peace isn't something I ask for — it's something I *create*.

I'm still growing, still healing, still glowing — but now I do it in a way that centers me, not the chaos around me.
If that makes me distant, quiet, or different? So be it.
My peace comes first.
That's not selfish. It's sacred.

## *A Letter to My Busy Self*

Dear Me,

You do not have to say yes just to feel seen.
You do not have to keep going just because they are watching.
You do not have to carry the entire world to prove you are strong.

You are not lazy for resting.
You are not selfish for saying no.
You are not behind —
you are becoming.

Some people will only notice you when you are running on empty.
Do not let their expectations become your standard.
You do not owe anyone full access to your
time, your energy, or your spirit.

You are more than your résumé.
More than your involvement list.
More than the things you produce.

You can pause.
You are allowed to walk away. You
are allowed to choose peace —
every single time.

Keep shining. But not at the cost of your glow.

Love,
Rayvn

# Chapter 14: The Group Chat

# Don't Know Everything

Now listen — I love a good group chat. I love a 2 AM call with the homies while we are on the game, venting, laughing, and just doing life together. But at one point, I had to ask myself: why do I feel like I owe everyone in my contacts an update? Why do I feel like I have to share what I am doing, fear, or what moves I am trying to make before I have made them?

There was a time when I shared everything. I thought it meant connection. I thought it meant being real. But the older I get, the more mysterious I try to be. Sometimes, oversharing does not come from a place of honesty — it comes from fear. I was scared to stand in silence. I did not know how to just *be* without commentary.

One thing I have learned? Every update does not need an audience. Growth is quiet. Healing is sacred. And it took me a while to realize that. **What I used to think was secrecy was strategy**. Some of the best moves I have ever made came from keeping my mouth shut and my head down. I took an entire year off social media and came back like I never left. Nobody even knew what I was building, what I was working on, or how hard I was praying.

There were moments during that break when I wanted to post my wins. I wanted to say, "Look at what I did!" Not even for validation — just because I was proud. But I had to stop and think, I do not know who is watching. I do not know who is clapping and who is secretly hoping I fail. So, I asked God to keep any evil intentions far away from me. I asked Him to cover me, even when I did not know what I needed protecting from.

When I needed space, I took it. I changed my number and deleted social media. For two whole months, nobody had access to me. I gave nobody my number. I went to school, came home, and minded my business. (Funny enough, I did not even know my iCloud location was still showing lol.)

But when I came back, I felt the love. My friends did not question me or make me feel guilty. They understood. They knew life happens. They knew silence is not always a cry for help — sometimes, it is just peace. I am so glad they did not take it as me acting funny or switching up. I was not. I was just protecting something I had not figured out yet.

When you are growing, especially growing aloud, it is easy for people to feel entitled to your process.

But you are not a reality show. This is not *Keeping Up with Rayvn's World*. Not everybody deserves access to who you are becoming.

When you are walking with God, when you are getting your life together, when you are resetting your mentality — things hit different. You might be in a soft season. Not because something is wrong, but because you finally have peace. And that peace? It does not need to be posted. It does not need to be shared in pieces or told through stories.

Discernment is self-care. There's power in saying, "I'm not ready to share this yet." Or "That's for me and God to discuss." You do not have to explain everything. You do not have to give away your process just to feel seen.

We always talk about protecting our energy, but do not forget to protect your peace, your plans, and your process, too. Not all ears are safe. Some people only listen so they can repeat. Others may love you, but they project their fears onto your future
— and that will mess you up if you are not grounded.

So, I stepped back. Not because I did not love my people. I love them deeply, but I needed to trust myself more. I needed to learn how to move without needing approval.

Now? Let them scroll past my silence and assume. Let them wonder about my glow-up. Let them guess where I have been. The real ones do not need proof — they *feel* it.

Matter of fact… I did not even tell anybody I was writing this book. By the time this hits your hands — by the time it has been published, posted, and out in the world, *that's* when people will find out.

That is how much I protected this season.

That is how sacred this was to me.
Because I do not play about me.
And God do not play about me.
**Peridot.**

*A Letter to Myself*

Dear Me,

You do not have to explain your silence.

You do not have to prove your progress.
You do not have to post every win just to be valid.
And you do not owe anyone a front-row seat to your healing.

What you are building in private is just as powerful as anything done in the spotlight.
The soft seasons count too. The moments when you disappear to protect your peace — they matter.
And the way you show up for yourself, even in stillness? That is a strength.

You are not distant. You are discerning.
You're not hiding. You are healing.
You're not being secretive — you are being sacred with your journey.

So, keep going. Keep choosing peace over performance.
Keep trusting God more than you trust people's opinions.

Because you do not play about you.
And God do not play about you either.

**Love,**

**The version of you. That is finally at peace**

# Chapter 15: Yes, I Belong Here

Let's talk about something real: imposter syndrome.

 Imposter syndrome is when you start doubting your skills, talent, or success — even when the proof is right in front of you. It is the voice in your head that says:

"You're not good enough."
"You don't belong here."
"They're going to figure out you're not really that smart."
It makes you feel like a fraud... even when you have done the work. Let me tell you — imposter syndrome in college? It hits differently. It will sneak up on you when you are sitting in class, walking into an internship, or just trying to finish a group project without losing your mind.

For me, chemistry was the moment imposter syndrome got LOUD.

Storytime: Before freshman year, I was taking college-level biology(I was majoring in biology then). I ended up switching to engineering (which was the right move for me), but since I am still in STEM, I had to take chemistry.

Whew.

I took chemistry in the fall of my freshman year, and let me tell y'all… I was not ready. I had my friend JoJo with me and listen —If you can survive chemistry with your friend, y'all are locked in for life.

We both ended up dropping the class at the same time.

Not because we did not care. But because we kept telling ourselves we could not do it.
We would say stuff like:

"Girl, this ain't clicking."
"We don't get it."
"Let's just drop it and try again later." We
let the fear talk louder than the facts.
The truth? We were both good at science. Always had been.
But because this was new, faster, and harder, we kept convincing ourselves we were not capable.

That's imposter syndrome.
It does not just show up in classrooms. It shows up in the mirror.
It will have you talking yourself out of spaces that were already yours.

Fall semester? Dropped.
Tried again sophomore year? Dropped again.
We did not fail the class — we just did not give ourselves a chance to finish it.

But guess what?
Spring semester of sophomore year? We passed.
We finally sat down, committed to it, and saw it through.
As wild as it sounds, once we got deeper into the course, it got easier.

The material was possible. We just finally applied ourselves instead of quitting too early.

Looking back, we just kept talking ourselves out of trying.

When the right professor came along — someone who explained it, cared, and believed in us, that made all the difference. That professor was heaven-sent, and the timing could not have been more perfect.

Sometimes, God waits until the moment you stop forcing it and start believing it.

So, what is the point?

Imposter syndrome had me in a chokehold, but it was never about what I could or could not do.

It was about what I kept telling myself
I could do it.
I knew science.
I knew I was smart.
But the minute it did not feel familiar, I started to doubt everything I already knew.

How many of us do that?

We walk into spaces — classrooms, meetings, internships, interviews — and instead of saying "I'm ready," we start thinking "I hope they don't find out I'm not ready."

The truth is: You would not be in the room if you did not already belong.

You would not have applied if you did not believe you had what it took.
You would not have gotten accepted if they had not seen something in you.

So, this is your reminder:

You do not have to shrink just because the room feels big.
You do not have to overcompensate to prove that you belong.
You do belong here.

And once you stop second-guessing yourself, that is when everything starts falling into place.

## *A Letter to Myself*

Dear Me,

You are not here by accident.

You earned your place —
every seat, every scholarship, every yes.
The moments you doubted yourself?
They were not proof that you did not
belong... They were proof that you cared.
That you were growing.
That you were stepping into something bigger.

You do not have to apologize for being smart.
You do not have to shrink just because
the room feels unfamiliar.
You do not have to keep proving
what has already been confirmed.

You are not a mistake.
You are not a fraud.
You are not too much.

You are fully equipped.
Fully capable.
And fully worthy of the spaces
you are walking into.

So next time your voice shakes
or your stomach turns,
Breathe. Stand up straight.
And say it with your chest:

"Yes, I belong here."

**Love,**
**The version of you**
**who knows that now**

# Chapter 16: Purpose Finds You Through People

I have had a lot of people show up for me in life — some for a moment, some for a season. But when **Sierra** (aka **Stevie**) came into my life, it felt different. Things that used to feel confusing started making sense. Questions I did not even know how to ask suddenly had answers. And most of all, I finally had someone who *saw me* in a way I had not even seen myself yet.

This chapter is dedicated to her.

No matter what anyone says, you need at least **one mentor** in your life.
Especially in your professional journey.
Especially as a Black woman navigating unfamiliar territory.
Especially when you are the *only one* in your family or your friend group walking a certain path.

I met Stevie back in **February of my freshman year**. I had been applying to different programs during the fall, just trying to get myself out there. Eventually, I heard back from a **company that had a mentoring program for HBCU students.**

The program itself was only a month or two long, but toward the end, they assigned us mentors.

And listen... they could not have matched me with a better person.

The first time we met, it was instant. We clicked so fast. There was no awkwardness, no pressure to perform, and I was comfortable to the point where I started being myself. Sierra met me right there. The energy was effortless.

We were only supposed to meet twice as part of the program. But I told her straight up:

> **"You are going to be my mentor. I'll call you in two weeks."**

I was not asking. I was *declaring it* — because I needed her. I needed someone who could guide me through this engineering world, which can feel like a maze when you do not have a map.

My sister's degree is in biology, and my mother's is in psychology. I am the only one in my family over here in engineering, and if my dad were still here, I know he would have helped me in every way possible. But navigating that first semester without guidance?

It was hard.
I did not know where to turn.
I did not have anyone who could break it down for me.

So, when I told Sierra she was my mentor, I was not joking. And she did not hesitate to say okay.

Since then, she has been like a big sister to me.

Whenever I have a question about opportunities, career moves, applications, or networking, she is always there. Her time zone is an hour ahead of mine, but she still makes time. She shows up. She supports me. She *guides*.

And it is not just about my field.
Sierra has become family. A consistent voice in a season of major change.
She's one of the best things that has happened to me since starting college — and I mean that with my whole heart.

The beautiful part is, by the time this book is out, I will have *finally* met her in person. We have known each other for over a year, but it is going to feel like a reunion, not having to be on FaceTime (I might cry). That is how deep our bond already is. She is the Stevie Wonder to my Ray Charles (that's an inside joke for us lol).

Mentorship is not just about career success.
It's about *alignment*.
It's about having someone who says,

> "Let me walk with you through this — because I've been there, and I believe in where you're going."

That is Sierra.
And she deserves her flowers.

## *A Letter to Sierra*

Dear Sierra,

From the very first time we spoke, I knew you were sent into my life for a reason. You didn't just arrive; you fit effortlessly. You understood me deeply. You created space for me to be myself. You recognized something special within me long before I could articulate it, and for this, I will forever thank God for aligning our paths.

You have been so much more than a mentor. You've been a big sister, a guiding light, and a constant reminder that I am never alone in this journey. From my freshman year, now going into my third year of college, you have stood by my side. You've guided me not only academically and professionally but through the complexities of growing up and learning to navigate adulthood.

There have been countless moments of uncertainty and confusion where I didn't even know the right questions to ask or the next steps to take, yet you were always there, patient and present. Because of you, I've never had to face any challenge feeling alone. You've supported me unconditionally, offering your wisdom and love freely, wholeheartedly, and consistently.

I hope you understand the magnitude of your impact on my life... not just professionally, but personally as well. You've inspired me to walk confidently, lead intentionally, and uplift others the way you've consistently uplifted me.

Please know that every accomplishment I celebrate, every new room I enter, and every goal I achieve carries a piece of you within it. Your influence shapes my actions, strengthens my decisions, and empowers me to move forward with courage and purpose.

Thank you for your time.

Thank you for your wisdom.

Thank you for simply being you.

I love you endlessly.

You are truly the blueprint.

Whenever I hear *Lean on Me* by Bill Withers, I think of you.
God knew I needed someone.
God knew I needed *you*.
**"A friend loves at all times, and a sister is born for adversity."**
**— Proverbs 17:17**
I pray you always know the impact you've had — not just on me,
but on every life you've touched.
This journey wouldn't feel complete without thanking you for all
you have done.

With all my love and gratitude,

**Rayvn**

# Chapter 17: Family First, But Me Too

When I left for college, I was scared (like most freshmen are), it was unfamiliar—a whole new world. My sister was still attending at the time (she was a junior, but school had always been like that for us). We had been in different grades, at the same school, walking two different paths, but this time felt different.

I missed my mommy.
Like... bad lol.

There were so many moments where I felt like I wanted to stay home just to be with her. But of course, my mama, being my mama, said,

**"Girl, what do you need to do that for?"**

My mom has always been the definition of strength. A strong, independent woman. I admire her deeply. I admire her circle. Her consistency. Her foundation. But she is also the foundation of my entire world. Even though my daddy is not here anymore, I give him credit too, because together, they raised two strong, independent girls. I love them both so much. I know if my father were here, he would be so proud of me.

That is why it was hard to leave.

Because I did not want to be far from the woman who raised me into everything I am.

I was lucky, though. I still had my sister on campus. While I love her, she had been away at school for two years, and I only saw her during holidays. Now that I was at school too, our days were still busy, but she always found time to stop by my room (mostly to see Rocky lol) and just check in (I love her for that).

I will never forget almost missing my mama's birthday. She told me it was fine. But I drove five hours just to pop up and surprise her (at the time, I was scared to drive on the interstate for personal reasons). I could not let the day pass without showing her love. That is what family means to me.

Still, it is not easy.

Family expectations vs. college reality?
Whew.

I have ADHD, so if I do not do something now, I am bound to forget. And in college, there is *always something* happening. Homework. Events. Classes. Deadlines. Two jobs. Three orgs. Mentorship meetings. It is a lot.

And then here comes the family questions:

- "When are you coming home this weekend?"
- "Are you staying down there for the break?"

- "Did you call your cousin back?"

- "Did you tell your Auntie Happy Birthday?"

Like I said, I am *not* a first-gen student. But I have seen the weight my friends carry trying to juggle school while staying accessible to their whole family. And I feel it too.

Sometimes I was just *too tired* to pick up the phone.
Sometimes I missed events.
Not because I did not care.
But because I was drained. Mentally. Emotionally. Physically.

But you know what? I am grateful.

I still go out to eat for my birthday every year — and though it used to be with my family back home, now it is with my college family. They make it feel just as special. My daddy used to always take me out to eat for my birthday, right up until his last days. So, continuing that tradition still means something to me, even in a new place.

I love my family more than ever...
But I also love *myself.*

I am grateful my mama understands that. With her doctorate and her wisdom, she gets the educational toll this takes. Some nights, I do not call her until 10 PM — but she still answers. Still shows up. Still reminds me that I am doing the best I can.

This is only Phase One.

Because I plan to retire my mama by the time I graduate.

I'm claiming that.

I believe that.

And I am walking toward it every day.

*Letter to My Family*

To the people who have seen me grow in every
form, this one is for you.

Mama, thank you. For being the glue, the strength, and the softness
I did not know I needed. You held me down when I could not even
hold myself. You never pushed me too far — you let me breathe
but always reminded me that I was built for more.

You are not just my mother — you are my foundation, my favorite
person, and my why. I love you beyond measure.

Daddy... I carry you with me every single day. Even in your
absence, your lessons echo in my spirit. I know you would be
proud of me — of the way I fight for myself, how I keep
showing up, and how I try to lead with love like you always did.

Thank you for raising a girl who could stand tall on her own but
still be soft enough to feel.

To my sister, you are my built-in best friend. My reminder that I
am never truly alone. Even when we are caught up in our worlds,
you always make space for me.

Thank you for being a light in mine.

I may not always call back right away or show up to every function, but trust and believe I carry y'all with me. Every success I have, I carry our name with it.

College taught me that love sometimes looks like distance.

It looks like missed calls and late-night texts, but also like relentless motivation and the drive to build something greater — for all of us.

For the legacy we carry.

I may not have said it enough… but I love y'all deeply.
And I am doing this for *us*.

Love always,
**Rayvn**

# Chapter 18: Legacy Loading

### *"I'm not done; I'm just getting started."*

If you have made it this far, pause.
Not for me — for *you*.

Whether you realize it or not, you have grown. You have reflected. Maybe you saw yourself in these chapters. Maybe it's your future self you're still figuring out. Either way, you showed up. For yourself.

And that? That is legacy.

See, when I used to hear the word "legacy," I thought it meant you had to be famous. Make history. Be some larger-than-life figure with a million accolades.

But as I have grown, and especially through my HBCU experience, I have learned that legacy is not about being known by everyone. It is about being known by the right ones and being true to yourself.

Legacy is what you leave behind when you walk out of the room. It's the way your friends talk about you when you are not there. It's the people who look up to you because of your resilience, even when they do not know the whole story.

For the introverted girls, the soft-spoken ones, the ones who used to hide in the back of the classroom, who avoided the spotlight, your legacy is *not* quiet just because *you* are.

It is written in the way you overcame.
In the goals you accomplished while doubting yourself.
In the way you healed without making a big announcement about it.
In the way, you still chose kindness, even after people hurt you.

You do not have to have all the answers right now. But what you *do* have is the power to shape what your story looks like.
You are your ancestors' wildest dreams.
You are your younger self's answered prayer.
You are *becoming* — and that becoming is the legacy.

I think about who I want to be when I leave my mark on this world. Not just in my career. Not just through my degree. But in the hearts of the people I have loved, supported, encouraged, and prayed for.

You have no idea how many people are watching you — quietly rooting for you.

How many girls will one day say, "She inspired me."

That is legacy.

Keep writing it, even when your hands shake.
Keep building it, even when the foundation feels shaky.
Keep owning it, even when no one is clapping yet.

Because one day,

Someone will pick up this book,
Read my story and see themselves.

And my legacy will have already reached them.

***Final Letter: To the Girl***

***Who Started This Journey***

You were tired. Nervous. Unsure.

But you were also brave.

You did not know exactly where you were going —

but you chose to begin anyway.

And through all the mess, the setbacks, the heartbreaks,

the questions, the long nights… You kept going.


You grew into someone your younger self

would be proud of.

You built something out of silence.

You found your rhythm, your people, your voice.

You created a home within yourself.

So, to the girl who started this journey:

Don't stop now.

Your legacy is loading —

And it is already beautiful.

You're not behind.

You are right on time.

Always,

**Rayvn**

# Now It's Your Turn...

Throughout this book, you have seen me take the time to write letters to myself, to my mentor, to my family. These letters helped me process where I was, where I am going, and how far I have already come. Writing them made me pause, reflect, and breathe.

Now, I want *you* to do the same.

Whether you are just starting your first year, transferring, or simply entering a new season, this is your moment to speak life into your future self. Do not hold back. Be honest. Be soft. Be real.

You might not feel like "her" just yet...
But she is already in you.

# Dear Future Me...

**Date:** _____

**Dear Future Me,**

_____

_____

_____

_____

_____

_____

_____

_____

_____

**With love,**
**Me.**

# Acknowledgments

To the readers — thank you. Whether you are an introvert, an HBCU student, or just someone trying to find your way, this book was written with you in mind. I hope these words made you feel seen, heard, and understood. I hope you remember that even in silence, your presence matters.

To my mentors, friends, and God — thank you for walking with me through every chapter of this journey. For every late-night conversation, every affirmation, every moment where I felt lost and was gently guided back — I am forever grateful.

To myself — thank you for not giving up. Thank you for choosing to heal, to write, to grow.

# Rayvn's Healing Playlist

These are a few songs that are in my playlist. I am sure y'all would enjoy them too.

- Jazmine Sullivan – Heaux Tales (entire album)
- India. Arie – Get It Together, Brown Skin, There's Hope
- Cat Burns – Free
- Sam Smith – Love Me More
- Beyoncé – All Night
- Lauryn Hill – Tell Him
- Jill Scott – Golden
- GloRilla – What You Know About Me, Let Her Cook
- Kendrick Lamar – Squabble Up
- Latto – Big Mama
- Flo Milli – Never Lose Me
- Megan Thee Stallion – Her, Anxiety
- JT – OKAY
- SZA – Good Days
- Kari Jobe + Tasha Cobbs Leonard – I am Getting Ready
- Mary Mary – Go Get It
- Yebba – Stand
- Tye Tribbett – He Turned It
- Kirk Franklin – Smile
- Tasha Cobbs Leonard – Break Every Chain
- Good Days – SZA
- Moment – Victoria Monét
- On My Mama – Victoria Monét
- ICU – Coco Jones
- Pressure – Ari Lennox
- New Apartment – Ari Lennox

- Get It Together – India. Arie
- Brown Skin – India. Arie
- Golden – Jill Scott
- Blessed – GloRilla
- Her – Megan Thee Stallion
- Anxiety – Megan Thee Stallion
- Big Mama – Latto
- Never Lose Me – Flo Milli
- Conceited – Flo Milli
- I am Getting Ready – Tasha Cobbs Leonard ft. Nicki Minaj
- Encourage Yourself – Donald Lawrence
- Won't He Do It – Koryn Hawthorne
- You Know My Name – Tasha Cobbs Leonard
- More Than I Can Bear – Kirk Franklin
- Deliver Me (This Is My Exodus) – Donald Lawrence & Le'Andria Johnson

Yes, I know some of these are a little auntie-coded, but every song has a season.

# Scriptures That Got Me Through

These scriptures have been a light for me through some of the hardest and most beautiful parts of my college journey. I hope they speak to your spirit the way they have to mine.

- **Philippians 4:13** *"I can do all things through Christ who strengthens me."* This one stays in my notes and in my heart. Period.
- **Jeremiah 29:11** *"For I know the plans I have for you, declares the Lord..."* A reminder that the confusion and chaos still have purpose.
- **Psalm 46:5** *"God is within her, she will not fall."* Say it again for the girls in the back.
- **Proverbs 3:5-6** *"Trust in the Lord with all your heart..."* Because faith > fear, every time.
- **Romans 8:28** *"And we know that all things work together for good..."* Even the setbacks. Even the losses. Even the silent seasons.
- **2 Timothy 1:7** *"For God has not given us a spirit of fear..."* Walk boldly. Even if your voice shakes.

- **Isaiah 41:10** *"So do not fear, for I am with you..."* When you feel alone, read this one aloud.
- **Isaiah 26:3** *"You will keep in perfect peace all who trust in you, all whose thoughts are fixed on you."* Mindset matters. Peace is my priority.
- **Galatians 6:9** *"Let us not become weary in doing good, for at the proper time we will reap a harvest if we do not give up."* Your effort is not in vain.
- **Romans 8:18** *"The pain that you've been feeling can't compare to the joy that's coming."* There is more on the way. Stay grounded.
- **Philippians 1:6** *"He who began a good work in you will carry it on to completion..."* Your glow-up is protected and in progress.
- **Ecclesiastes 3:1** *"To everything there is a season, and a time to every purpose under heaven."* Trust the timing, even in transition.

# Author's Note

I wrote this book for the girls who move in silence. For the ones who sit in the back of the room, but whose presence still carries weight. This is for you — to remind you that you can make a significant impact without changing who you are.

I have come a long way on this journey. I know they are proud of me, and I know my dad would be especially proud of the young woman he raised, up until it was his time to go.

To my mother and Rayna — thank you for keeping me grounded, focused, and on the right path. I have not got my whole life figured out, but I am surrounded by love and support that pushes me to be better every day.

To Sierra, my amazing mentor. You have taught me that I can make an impact just by being me. Thank you for everything.

And to Camryn — my light. Shine down on me constantly.

With love,
**Rayvn**

# About the Author

Rayvn Webster is a Memphis native and current student at Jackson State University in Jackson, Mississippi. As a young Black woman majoring in engineering, Rayvn is passionate about building, creating, and innovating — not just through technology, but through impact. Her dream has always been to give back to the younger generation, especially girls like her who move quietly but carry a big purpose.

Rayvn combines her love for storytelling, leadership, and service to inspire other HBCU introverts to step into their light, on their terms. She hopes this book reminds you that being "quiet" does not mean being invisible, and that sometimes the ones who sit in the back are the ones with the loudest power.

When she is not writing, creating, or taking care of Rocky (her emotional support pup), you can find her enjoying time with her friends and family, journaling, and pouring back into her community — one step, one prayer, and one goal at a time.